This book belongs to

Delectables
For All Seasons

Maryjo Koch

Tea

SWANS ISLAND BOOKS

CollinsPublishersSanFrancisco
A Division of HarperCollins*Publishers*

PUBLISHED IN 1995 BY
COLLINS PUBLISHERS SAN FRANCISCO
1160 BATTERY STREET
SAN FRANCISCO CA 94111

SWANS ISLAND BOOKS

LIBRARY OF CONGRESS CATALOGING-IN-PUBLICATION DATA

KOCH, MARYJO
      TEA: DELECTABLES FOR ALL SEASONS / MARYJO KOCH
         P. CM.
      "SWANS ISLAND BOOKS"
      ISBN 0-00-255480-1
      1. TEA.   2. HERBAL TEAS.
TX817.T3K63   1995
641.6'372 — DC20   94-30914
                                    CIP

PRINTED IN HONG KONG
10 9 8 7 6 5 4 3 2 1

Ocha o iremasu.
I make tea for you.

EA

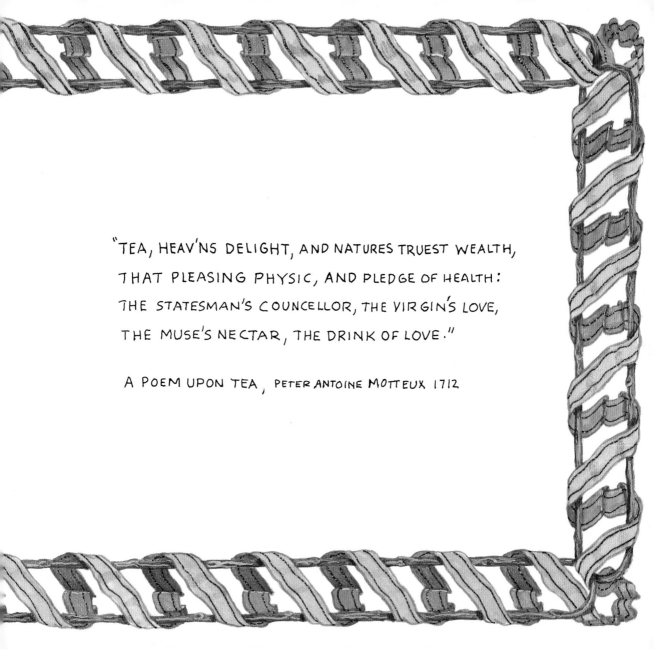

"TEA, HEAV'NS DELIGHT, AND NATURES TRUEST WEALTH,
THAT PLEASING PHYSIC, AND PLEDGE OF HEALTH:
THE STATESMAN'S COUNCELLOR, THE VIRGIN'S LOVE,
THE MUSE'S NECTAR, THE DRINK OF LOVE."

A POEM UPON TEA, PETER ANTOINE MOTTEUX 1712

THE DIVINE SHRUB: THE QUEEN OF CAMELLIAS

An immediate sense of intimacy is evoked by the contemplation of a cup of tea. Indeed, everything about the life cycle of the bushy evergreen Camellia sinensis evokes the dewy temperate mists under which it thrives, for the plant is cultivated not on a plantation or a farm, but in a "garden."

The world's finest tea gardens, from the Far East to West Africa, have in common pure mountain breezes and sunny days followed by rainy nights. Each of these is fundamental in the production of exquisite teas with the most subtle fragrance.

The plants are generally grown from cuttings from a parent plant, thus assuring noble lineage. After three years the plants become productive and can remain so for a century.

In Asia, only women harvest the jasmine-like scented plants. According to some local traditions their agility, patience, and accuracy are uniquely "feminine" traits essential to nurturing tea to its full charm.

TEA LEAVES ARE READY TO BE PICKED OR "PLUCKED" FOR HARVEST WHEN THE YOUNG SHOOTS APPEAR. IN MOST REGIONS PLUCKING IS SEASONAL, BUT IN THE HOTTEST CLIMATES, IT IS A YEAR-ROUND ENDEAVOR. BUSHES ARE PLUCKED BETWEEN THREE AND TWELVE TIMES A YEAR, WITH THE SECOND PLUCKING THE MOST DESIRABLE.

AN INFUSION OF FRESH TEA LEAVES WOULD BE HARSH, RAW AND THIN. THE FINISHED CHARACTER OF THE DRY LEAF IS DETERMINED BY THE FERMENTATION PROCESS, JUST AS GRAPES ARE TRANSFORMED INTO MATURE WINE. CAREFUL STEPS AND PROCEDURES OXIDIZE THE LEAVES AND CHANGE THEIR CHEMISTRY.

THE LEAVES ARE DRIED BY WITHERING, THAT IS, BY SPREADING THEM OUT FOR UP TO ONE FULL DAY ON RACKS MADE OF THIN CLOTH STRETCHED TAUTLY OVER A WIRE-MESH FRAME. NEXT, THE LEAVES ARE ROLLED BY TOSSING THEM IN BASKETS, A PROCESS THAT MACERATES THEM AND RELEASES THEIR JUICES. WHILE THE LEAVES FERMENT THEY BEGIN TO DARKEN AND THE AIR FILLS WITH A FRAGRANCE SIMILAR TO APPLE BLOSSOMS.

FINALLY, FIRING HALTS FURTHER FERMENTATION. SIMILAR TO STIR-FRYING, FIRING IS TRADITIONALLY CARRIED OUT IN LARGE METAL WOKS OVER A ROARING FIRE, OR INDUSTRIALLY IN LARGE OVENS.

THE DRIED LEAVES ARE THEN SORTED BY GRADE INTO LOOSE TEA, BROKEN LEAVES, AND FANNINGS, OR LEAF DUST, USED IN TEA BAGS.

Origin Myths: Mystical Alchemy

Legend has it that in ancient China, heaven and earth were split assunder to give birth to the world. With the help of the sovereigns, the emperors of earth, heaven, and mankind invented all the arts and crafts, which they then presented to men.

Shen Nung, one of the sovereigns, the divine cultivator, was the first to till the earth. One day, while this inventor of herbal medicine, alchemy, and agriculture was tending his garden, he burned a camellia bush and marveled at the aroma that assailed him. A shiny, dark green leaf fell into the pot of water which he was boiling. Sampling the golden elixir he declared it divine and presented man with the gift of tea.

Tea Garden Tales

Reminiscent of Rudyard Kipling's tales from the Jungle Book, stories from Assam reveal the isolation of the first Indian tea gardens and the pioneering spirit of the planters.

A Giant Garden Snake

Unexpectedly, while clearing a small patch of forest to plant tea, the workers dropped their tools and fled. The puzzled sidar, the foreman, inquired what the panic was about. "Sir," they replied, "there is a very large snake!" The sidar, clambering up on top of a large fallen trunk to locate the viper amongst the timber, shouted, "Can you point to where you last sighted it?" "Sir," they called from an even greater distance, "you are standing on the python."

Tiger Sam

ALL THE JUNGLE BEASTS SHARED WITH MOTHER NATURE
THEIR RESENTMENT AT HAVING THEIR RUSTIC FURNITURE
DISTURBED BY THE CLAMOR AND ORDER OF THE TEA GARDENS. ONE
EVENING THREE PLANTERS WERE DOZING ON THE VERANDA,
HAVING DRUNK SOMETHING STRONGER THAN TEA AT DINNER. A
SUDDEN CRY AWOKE TWO OF THE MEN. A PROWLING TIGER,
DETERMINED TO TAKE MATTERS INTO HIS OWN PAWS, HAD DRAGGED
THE THIRD MAN FROM THE TERRACE. ONE OF THE DAZED
PLANTERS CAME QUICKLY TO HIS SENSES, AND WARDED OFF
THE ATTACK. HE BECAME KNOWN AS THE HEROIC TIGER SAM.

All the Tea in China

Tea epitomizes the Chinese understanding of the cyclical nature of time and change, celebration and ceremony.

首日封 F.D.C.

宜兴紫砂陶
1994·5·5
北京

The ancient popularity of tea in China was a catalyst for cultural development. The act of drinking tea was to be attended by a reverence for nature and beauty. Lu Yuan, a ninth-century vagabond turned scholar, recognized the same harmony and flow that ordered the entire universe in the simplicity and beauty of the tea service. He undertook the writing of the Ch'a Ching, the classic of tea, in which he codified the known world of tea. The work became a landmark in Taoist thought and would later inspire the Japanese tea ceremony.

"... *I* HAVE NEVER TASTED TEA LIKE THIS. IT IS SMOOTH,
PUNGENT, AND INSTANTLY ADDICTING ... THIS IS FROM GRAND
AUNTIE, MY MOTHER EXPLAINS ... SHE TOLD ME 'IF I BUY
THE CHEAP TEA, THEN I AM SAYING THAT MY WHOLE LIFE
HAS NOT BEEN WORTH SOMETHING BETTER ... IF I BUY JUST
A LITTLE, THEN I AM SAYING THAT MY LIFETIME IS ALMOST
OVER,' SO SHE BOUGHT ENOUGH TEA FOR ANOTHER LIFETIME."

THE KITCHEN GOD'S WIFE, AMY TAN 1991

Medicine: Camellia Sinensis, Heady Remedies

"Better to be deprived of food for three days, than tea for one"

ANCIENT CHINESE PROVERB

As early as 3000 B.C., the Chinese considered tea a potent medicinal herb, as well as a delectable beverage.

Tips from the tea garden to your garden:

Green tea is rich in fluoride; it can reduce tooth decay and boost the immune system. Use a pad soaked in weak green tea to make an emergency first aid treatment to ease bleeding from cuts and grazes and to soothe insect bites.

Oolong tea, such as puerh, is effective in keeping fats soluble in the body, a characteristic which has earned it the nickname of the dieter's tea. Medical news from the Far East indicates that it is effective in reducing cholesterol in the blood.

Black tea can provide relief from too much tippling. Refresh tired eyes by placing damp black tea bags on closed eyelids. Wash with a weak infusion for relief from sunburn.

CERAMIC TEAPOTS TAKE ON A "LINING", OR ABSORB OILS AND

AND LEAVE THE LID OFF TO AVOID A MUSTY SMELL.

NEVER DRY THE INSIDE, INSTEAD, PUT A LUMP OF SUGAR IN THE BOTTOM

Garlic Tea is often touted for its effectiveness in fighting off colds.

In the first century, mint tea was recommended for hiccups by the Roman scholar Pliny the Elder.

Chamomile Tea is good for treating indigestion, insomnia, stress, and anxiety in poor weary little rabbits who have gotten into trouble (while pillaging their neighbors' vegetable patches). Mother Rabbit recommends "one table-spoonful to be taken at bed-time."

Fennel Tea, the nursing mother's companion, increases milk flow and relieves a baby's colic. Lavender tea calms cranky children.

St. John's Wort Tea expels demons, witches, and fairies.

Marigold Tea was recommended in the 1600's as a plague preventative and an essential ingredient in love potions.

Meadowsweet Tea, known to Hippocrates in the 4th century B.C. and later a popular Elizabethan tisane, was used to ease fever and pain. Anti-inflammatory chemicals called salicylates were extracted from meadowsweet in the 1830's. Sixty years later, the pharmaceutical company Bayer produced a similar substance artificially. They called the new wonder drug after its old botanical name, spiraea ulmaria, or aspirin.

Tisane The Herbal Pharmacopeia: Peter Rabbit's Cure

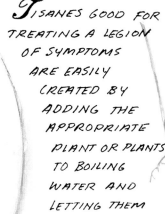

Without exception, every human culture has either an oral or written tradition which describes the therapeutic and healing properties of a vast variety of plants.

Tisanes good for treating a legion of symptoms are easily created by adding the appropriate plant or plants to boiling water and letting them brew or stew.

The line between herbs and spices in both ancient decoctions and contemporary infusions is vague and probably, in the end, of little importance.

Peter was not very well during the evening. His mother put him to bed,

and made some camomile tea; 'One table-spoonful to be taken at bed-time'

EAVES

..."So I must rise at early dawn, as busy as can be, to get my daily labor done, and pluck the leafy tea."

Ballad of the tea pickers   Le Yih, early Ch'ing Dynasty, 1644

AUTUMN

"HIGH IN THE LUBERON HILLS IN THE SOUTH OF FRANCE, NEAR THE ANCIENT VILLAGE OF BONNIEUX, THE FIRST TEA OF THE DAY IS BREWING, AS THE AUTUMN SUN WARMS THE MORNING... A STRONG GRAND YUNNAN TEA AWAKENS THE SENSES. A WIRE BASKET IS FILLED WITH FOUGASSE..... PIECES OF THE ROBUST PROVENCAL BREAD ARE BROKEN OFF AND DIPPED INTO THE TEA."

FRENCH TEA   CAROLE MANCHESTER
                                        1993

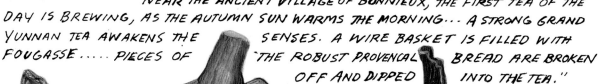

Mushroom Tea,
PERHAPS?

BEAUTIFUL ON A POT,
NOT IN IT.

Fougasse and Olives

2-¼-OUNCE PACKAGES ACTIVE DRY YEAST

3 TO 3 ½ CUPS BREAD FLOUR

1 CUP WARM WATER

1 CUP BUCKWHEAT FLOUR

1 TEASPOON SALT

1 TABLESPOON OLIVE OIL

½ POUND BLACK OLIVES, SUCH AS NICOISE OR KALAMATA, PITTED AND CHOPPED (ABOUT 1½ CUPS)

1 EGG BEATEN WITH 1 TEASPOON WATER AND A PINCH OF SALT, FOR EGG GLAZE

IN A BOWL, COMBINE THE YEAST, 1 CUP OF THE BREAD FLOUR, AND ½ CUP OF THE WATER AND BEAT UNTIL COMBINED. COVER WITH PLASTIC WRAP AND LET RISE IN A WARM PLACE FOR 1 HOUR.

TRANSFER TO A LARGE BOWL AND ADD THE REMAINING WATER, THE BUCKWHEAT FLOUR, SALT, OLIVE OIL, AND ENOUGH OF THE REMAINING BREAD FLOUR TO FORM A SOFT DOUGH. TURN THE DOUGH OUT ONTO A LIGHTLY FLOURED SURFACE AND KNEAD FOR 7 TO 8 MINUTES, OR UNTIL SMOOTH AND ELASTIC. TRANSFER TO AN OILED BOWL, TURN TO COAT WITH THE OIL, AND COVER WITH PLASTIC WRAP. LET RISE FOR 1 TO 1½ HOURS, OR UNTIL DOUBLED IN BULK.

PREHEAT THE OVEN TO 400° F. TURN THE DOUGH OUT ONTO A LIGHTLY FLOURED WORK SURFACE, AND KNEAD IT WELL. GRADUALLY KNEAD IN THE OLIVES. DIVIDE THE DOUGH IN HALF, AND FORM IT INTO 2 FLAT LOAVES. WITH THE POINT OF A SHARP KNIFE, MAKE SEVERAL SLASHES IN THE TOP OF EACH LOAF, PULLING THE DOUGH APART AT THE SLASHES. BRUSH THE TOPS OF THE LOAVES WITH THE EGG GLAZE, AND ARRANGE THE LOAVES ON A LIGHTLY FLOURED BAKING SHEET. BAKE FOR 30 TO 35 MINUTES, OR UNTIL THE TOPS OF THE LOAVES ARE GOLDEN BROWN AND THE BOTTOMS SOUND HOLLOW WHEN TAPPED. TRANSFER TO RACKS TO COOL. MAKES 2 LOAVES.

WATER FLOWERS

Japan: Cha-No-Yu

*"Ujini kite
Byobu ni nitaru
Chatsumi kana"*

*"A rare thing to see
Is a glimpse gathering tea
In Uji's fair scene;
As from bushes on a screen"*

HAIKU FREELY TRANSLATED FROM JAPANESE   ONITSURA, DATE UNKNOWN

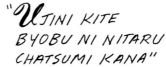

A cheerful letter on its way to you.

Walk silently and leave worldly noise behind as you cross the roji, the garden paving stones, damp with dew. Concentrate on the moss, trees, and birdsong outside the sukiya, the abode of vacancy, the teahouse.

Inside, observe the flowers, arranged to evoke coolness in the summer and warmth in the winter. Contemplate the sound of the water boiling, the simplicity of the room, and the movements of the host, which follow strict rules established centuries ago.

Meditate as the powdered green tea is whipped into a froth of liquid jade with a chasen, a delicately crafted bamboo whisk.

Sip the "precious treasure" from the thoughtfully chosen teacup and, together with the other honored guests, experience the harmony of nature and the art of life as it is idealized in the venerable cha-no-yu:

THE HOT WATER TEA CEREMONY.

Cup Tossing: Fortune Telling

A Few Tell Tale Leaves

THREE SMALL LEAVES NEXT TO A LARGE ONE
TWO LEAVES CLOSE TO A SMALL ONE
SMALL LEAVES IN A TRIANGULAR PATTERN
HEART PATTERN
TRIANGLE
SQUARE
STAR
MANY SCATTERED LEAVES
FLOWERS
TEAPOT
KEY
HOUSE
DOTS
DASHES
FRUIT
CIRCLE
SCISSORS
HAMMER

And The Tales They Tell

A MAN
A WOMAN
A CHILD
LOVE
JEALOUSY
SOLID CHARACTER
GREAT SUCCESS
EXTRAVAGANCE
JOY
GOOD CHEER
SECRETS
STABILITY
MESSAGES
SURPRISES
CHILDREN
CLOSE PARTNERSHIP
ANGRY WORDS
HARD WORK

According to occult lore, the bowl of the tea cup corresponds to the dome of the sky, and the tea leaves to the stars. The time-honored method for reading the leaves is simple. A client inverts his or her cup, turns it around three times, places it on a saucer, and taps the bottom with the left index finger. The reader, in a light trance of course, turns the cup over and studies the leaves.

COZIES

"The agony of the leaves" is the expression tea tasters use to describe the moment tea leaves begin to unfold in the teapot after furiously boiling water is poured on them.

Quickly covering the teapot with a cozy will guarantee a constant high temperature while the tea is brewing, and is the secret to obtaining the fullest "draw," or most flavorful infusion.

Winter White Tea

THIS IS SAID TO BE EFFECTIVE AGAINST SLEEPLESSNESS. IT IS INSPIRED BY THE "WHITE COFFEE" RECIPE OR KAHWAH BEIDA DRINK OF LEBANON. BUT MY MOTHER LOVED THE SCENT OF ORANGES (ALMOST AS MUCH AS ROSES!) SO SHE CALLED IT WINTER TEA. ON BLUSTERY COLD NIGHTS WE'D CLUTCH OUR STEAMING CUPS CLOSE TO OUR NOSES, SIPPING, STEAMING AND DREAMING OF SPRING.

FILL EACH GLASS OR DEMI-TASSE WITH HOT WATER AND ONE TEASPOON OF WHITE SUGAR. IF POSSIBLE, USE SMALL INDIVIDUAL PITCHERS FILLED WITH ORANGE FLOWER WATER AND LET EACH GUEST ADD EAU DE FLEURS AND SUGAR TO SUIT THEIR OWN TASTE. SERVE WITH PAPER-THIN ORANGE SLICES FOR EATING OR DOUSING INTO THE TEA CONCOCTION.

ORANGE FLOWER WATER
PRODUCED IN FRANCE
A. MONTEUX
PARFUMEUR + DISTILLATEU
VALLAURIS (Alpes Mmes)
NET WT. 6 2/3 OZ

WINTER

A STEAMING "WHITE TEA" IS ONE OF TWO SEASONAL DIVERSIONS THAT CAN EASE THE BITE OF ANY WINTER. THE OTHER IS SEED CATALOGS.

A WINTER WHITE TEA IS SERVED IN FROSTED ETCHED-GLASS CUPS AND CAN BE ACCOMPANIED BY MELT-IN-YOUR-MOUTH SNOWFLAKE MERINGUE COOKIES, SPRINKLED WITH SILVER ICE "PEARLS."

THE GOURMET'S GUIDE

Each day over three billion cups of tea are consumed world wide, making it second in consumption only to water. All of the planet's vast tea supply can be separated into three categories, which are simple variations in the processing of the singular tea plant. Black teas, semi-black, and oolong teas are rolled, withered, fermented, and dried for varying lengths of time, while green teas are only rolled and dried.

Black Teas

	Origin	Description
Darjeeling	Grown in the Himalayan foothills at 7000 feet!	Full-bodied, delicate, amber color, pleasant aftertaste.
Assam	From N.E. India and Pakistan, grown at low altitudes.	Robust, rich, cloudy, poor varieties are bitter.
Ceylon	From high altitudes of Sri Lanka.	Intense flavor, pleasant aroma, bright color.
Keemun	Grown in China and Taiwan, best of China's black tea.	Thick, superb bouquet, smooth, excellent with food.
Lapsang Souchong	From Hunan and Fukien provinces in China and Taiwan.	Strong, hearty, smoky flavor and aroma, sweet.

Semi-Black Teas

	Origin	Description
Oolong	Comes from Amoy, Foochow, and Canton in China and Taiwan.	Tea that looks and tastes like half-black and half-green tea, subtle, fruity, light color.

Green Teas	Origin	Description
GUNPOWDER	FROM TAIWAN AND CHINA.	BITTER, PUNGENT, YELLOW-GREEN.
HYSON	CHINESE GREEN TEA.	FRAGRANT, LIGHT, MELLOW.
GYOKURO	BEST JAPANESE EXPORTED TEA.	MILD, SLIGHTLY SWEET.
SENCHA	COMMON COMMERCIAL JAPANESE TEA.	SOOTHING, FRESH, USUALLY SERVED WITH SUSHI.

Purveyors of tea specialize in selling various blends as well as grades of tea. The Mariage Freres company in Paris sells over 350 blends created by specialists who mix the basic tea types in varying proportions and add myriad fruity, floral, or herbal essences. Master the basics, then blend your own according to whim and time of day. ...Store tea in an airtight tin to protect it from its enemies: air, light, heat, and humidity.

Blended Teas	Composition	Description
ENGLISH BREAKFAST	BLEND OF BLACK CHINA AND CEYLON TEAS.	FULL-BODIED, RICH, AND FRAGRANT.
IRISH BREAKFAST	BLEND OF BLACK TEA.	MEDIUM-STRONG.
RUSSIAN	BLEND OF BLACK CHINA TEA.	VERY STRONG AND DARK.

Blended and Scented Teas	Composition	Description
EARL GREY	BLENDED FROM INDIA AND CEYLON BLACK TEAS.	HEARTY AND AROMATIC.
ORCHID TEA	BLEND OF SEMI-FERMENTED OOLONG TEA WITH CRUSHED ORCHID FLOWERS.	LIGHT, DELICATE, AND FRAGRANT.

TEA TOTALER'S SELECTION

Herbal Teas

Proving that variety is the spice of life, tea lovers do not only use tea plants to make tea. The leaves, roots, and flowers of scores of plants are infused in boiling water to create tisanes, or herbal teas.

Herb	Flavor
BASIL	EXQUISITE AROMA, PEPPERY, AND CLOVELIKE.
CATNIP	AROMATIC AND MINTY (A FELINE FAVORITE).
CHAMOMILE	LIGHT APPLE FLAVOR.
CHICORY	COFFEELIKE, SLIGHTLY BITTER.
CHRYSANTHEMUM	ORIGINALLY DRIED FOR CHINESE EMPERORS, THESE FLOWERS PRODUCE A SLIGHTLY BITTER-SWEET TEA.
GINGER	SPICY WITH WARM AFTERTASTE, COMFORTING FOR COLDS.
GINSENG	THESE DRIED ROOTS, IMPORTED FROM THE ORIENT AND SOLD IN CHINESE HERB SHOPS FOR A LONG LIST OF ILLNESSES, MAKE A TEA THAT IS IMPROVED WITH SUGAR OR HONEY.

$\mathcal{H}$ERB	$\mathcal{F}$LAVOR
GOLDEN SEAL	GRASSY, SOUR, AND BITTER; OFTEN BLENDED WITH MINT, THYME, MARJORAM, OR BLACK TEA; YELLOW-GREEN COLOR.
HIBISCUS	SLIGHTLY TART AND LEMONY, PALE RUBY COLOR.
JASMINE	FRAGRANT AND SWEET.
LAVENDER	COOLING, DELICIOUS WITH GOOD BLACK TEA.
LEMON VERBENA	CITRUS FRAGRANCE, DELICIOUS WITH GOOD BLACK TEA.
LICORICE	SWEET, SATISFYING THIRST QUENCHER.
LIME	SIMILAR TO CHAMOMILE, APPLELIKE, SWEET AND AROMATIC.
PEPPERMINT	GREEN COLOR AND MINT FLAVOR, FRUITY, LESS FRAGRANT THAN SPEARMINT. USED TO SPICE OTHER HERBS AND TEAS.
RED RASPBERRY	ASTRINGENT AND AROMATIC.
STRAWBERRY	HIGH IN VITAMINS.
VALERIAN	SOOTHING, STRONGLY SCENTED, INDUCES SLEEP.
YERBA MATÉ	REFRESHING, CONTAINS CAFFEINE AND TANNIN, STIMULATING, GRASSY TASTE.

# REWING the BEST

A GREAT TEA GARDEN, CAREFUL PROCESSING, AND SKILLFUL BLENDING ARE ONLY THE BEGINNING OF THE JOURNEY TO A GREAT CUP OF TEA. FASTIDIOUS ATTENTION TO A FEW BREWING BASICS WILL BRING OUT THE ROMANCE OF THE LEAVES IN THE FINAL CUP. ASPIRING TEA MASTERS CAN THEN EXPLORE THE ENDLESS SUBTLETIES OF TEA IN A PERSONAL CEREMONY, LINGERING AND MUSING OVER EACH NUANCE OF THE TEA AND THE SERVICE.

Black and Green Teas

- USE A CLEAN, WARMED, WELL-SEASONED TEAPOT
- ADD ONE TEASPOON OF TEA LEAVES FOR EACH 6-OUNCE CUP OF TEA
- BRING FRESH, COLD WATER TO A ROLLING BOIL AND POUR IMMEDIATELY ON THE TEA LEAVES
- COVER AND LET TEA BREW FOR 3 TO 5 MINUTES
- STIR ONCE AND PROMPTLY POUR LIQUID OFF LEAVES.

Herbal Teas

MANY HERB TEAS HAVE FLAVOR, AROMA, AND APPEARANCE EQUAL TO THAT OF THE BEST IMPORTED TEAS. GROW HERBS IN WINDOW BOXES IN YOUR KITCHEN AND USE THEM FRESH.

BECAUSE THE FLAVOR OF FRESH HERBS IS LESS CONCENTRATED THAN THAT OF DRIED HERBS, YOU MUST USE GREATER AMOUNTS WHEN MAKING TEAS WITH THEM. WHEN USING DRIED LEAVES, ROOTS, OR SEEDS, USE TWO TEASPOONS OF HERBS TO EACH PINT OF BOILING WATER OR ONE TEASPOON TO EACH CUP.

THE BLOOM of the TASTE BUD

THE THORNY QUESTION REMAINS: DO THE TRUE CONNOISSEURS USE ADDITIVES IN THEIR TEA? TIME OF DAY AND REGIONAL PREFERENCES DO FACTOR INTO THE IMBIBERS' DEBATE, BUT ULTIMATELY, TASTE IS PERSONAL, ADVENTUROUS, MYSTERIOUS, AND SENSUOUS. THE MOST PROSAIC TEATOTALERS SWEAR BY BLACK TEA "STRONG ENOUGH TO TROT A MOUSE ON."

BLACK — UNADORNED, ESSENTIAL FOR ALL TYPES OF SMOKY OR SEMI-FERMENTED TEAS, SUCH AS DARJEELING, GREEN GUNPOWDER, AND LAPSANG SOUCHONG. IDEAL WITH SAVORY FOODS ANYTIME.

MILK — PARTICULARLY SUITABLE FOR MORNING TEAS, SUCH AS ASSAM OR CEYLON.

SUGAR — MARRIES WELL WITH MANY SCENTED TEAS, AS A SORT OF DESSERT.

HONEY — HARMONIOUS WITH MANY HERBAL TEAS; ADDS ITS OWN UNIQUE HEALING POWERS TO MANY REMEDIES WHILE CAMOUFLAGING BITTERNESS IN SOME.

LEMON — CHANGES THE TASTE AND COLOR OF TEA. CAN ENHANCE THE BOUQUET OF ASSAM OR CEYLON TEA. COCO CHANEL, THE FRENCH DESIGNER, ALWAYS TOOK HER TEA WITH LEMON.

JAM — RUSSIAN CARAVAN TEA, POURED FROM A SAMOVAR AND SERVED WITH A SPOONFUL OF STRAWBERRY OR CHERRY PRESERVES IN A GLASS.

ICED — A DOUBLE-STRENGTH INFUSION OF MOST TYPES OF TEA POURED OVER ICE IS THIRST QUENCHING AND REVITALIZING.

FORTIFIED — JULEPED WITH MINT LIQUEUR; CEYLON TEA PUNCH WITH RUM AND SHERRY, SPIKED AND ICED; TEA TODDIES WITH WHISKEY AND GINGER WINE. NAUGHTY BUT NICE.

SAVORY — HOT JAPANESE GREEN TEA IS POURED OVER LEFTOVER BREAKFAST RICE AND SALT-PRESERVED SEAFOOD.

BURMESE PICKLED TEA LEAVES AND ZAUNGY FRUIT ARE MIXED TOGETHER, SET ASIDE FOR TWO WEEKS, THEN GARNISHED WITH DRIED SHRIMP, SESAME SEEDS, FRIED GARLIC, SHREDDED COCONUT, AND ROASTED PEAS!

Small porcelain teacups without handles, and saucers with bowls sporting elaborately decorated covers arrived from China along with the first tea shipments, ideal as ballast in the ships' holds. Bending to European preference, China began to produce cups with handles. As tea prices dropped, cups grew larger.

Today those with more leisure time and two hands free tend

*R*USSIANS PREFERRED GLASS FOR DRINKING TEA "WITH THEIR EYES" AS WELL AS THEIR PALATES.

*T*HE CHINESE MYSTERY OF FABRICATING PORCELAIN WAS NOT UNLOCKED IN THE WEST UNTIL THE BEGINNING OF THE 18TH CENTURY, BY A PRUSSIAN ALCHEMIST.

TO FAVOR CUPS AND SAUCERS, WHILE THE BUSY MASSES USE MUGS.

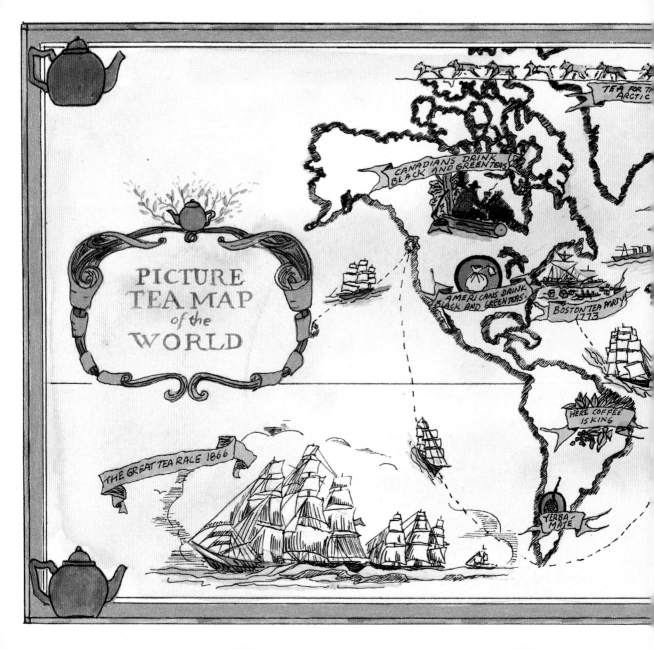

PICTURE
TEA MAP
of the
WORLD

TEA FOR THE ARCTIC

CANADIANS DRINK BLACK AND GREEN TEAS

AMERICANS DRINK BLACK AND GREEN TEAS

BOSTON TEA PARTY 1773

HERE COFFEE IS KING

YERBA-MATE

THE GREAT TEA RACE 1866

BOUQUET

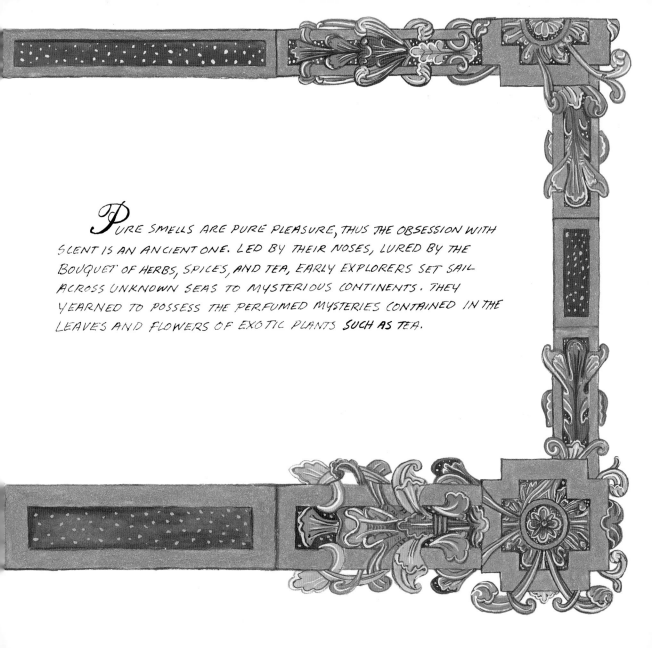

*P*URE SMELLS ARE PURE PLEASURE, THUS THE OBSESSION WITH SCENT IS AN ANCIENT ONE. LED BY THEIR NOSES, LURED BY THE BOUQUET OF HERBS, SPICES, AND TEA, EARLY EXPLORERS SET SAIL ACROSS UNKNOWN SEAS TO MYSTERIOUS CONTINENTS. THEY YEARNED TO POSSESS THE PERFUMED MYSTERIES CONTAINED IN THE LEAVES AND FLOWERS OF EXOTIC PLANTS **SUCH AS TEA.**

Floral teas - rose, jasmine, or chrysanthemum - can be festively served with biscuits and rose-petal butter, edible sugar-crystal violets, and other flower foods.

Candied Flowers

Delicate crystallized flowers are beautiful decorations for puddings, ice cream, cakes, fruit salads or just to crunch on their own while sipping a comforting tisane and reading a romantic novel or a love letter. Use tiny rose buds, pinks, rose petals, violets, mimosa, lilacs, fruit or herb flowers and mint leaves. It must be done on a very dry day. Pick the flowers, remove all stems and green, trim the white heels from rose petals and pinks. Wash and dry them thoroughly.

Beat 2 or more egg whites until frothy. Paint each flower, leaf or petal with the egg white with a clean, soft paint brush, then hold with tweezers and dip each one into sugar and make sure that they are completely coated. Place on a baking sheet or tray and dry them in an airing cupboard or warm oven with the door ajar. When all your flowers are dry, place them between sheets of waxed paper in boxes or tins.

Spring

TO SEE A HILLSIDE WHITE WITH DOGWOOD BLOOM IS TO KNOW A PARTICULAR ECSTASY OF BEAUTY, BUT TO WALK THE GRAY WINTER WOODS AND FIND THE BUDS WHICH WILL RESURRECT THAT BEAUTY IN ANOTHER MAY IS TO PARTAKE OF CONTINUITY

HAL BORLAND, THE NEW YORK TIMES, NOVEMBER 29 1948

England: Tip Me Over, Pour Me Out.

For the english, tea is more than a tradition: it is a way of life. With the exception of china, great britain is the largest tea-consuming nation in the world. The story of its rise from oriental obscurity to coffeehouse curiosity to absolute necessity is a tale of global commerce, subterfuge, and politics. Armed with rapier wit and dandy style, tea's proponents fought their genteel battles with coffee-lovers in the empire's drawing rooms. The leaf beat the bean soundly in england's affections.

Each strata of British society has its own habits and habitats. Tea can be had at tea rooms, tea shops, tea houses, tea gardens, tea dances, tea stalls, tea wagons, and on tea trolleys.

Tea at every corner of the kingdom

In the rural north of England, high tea is still served in the late afternoon. This early evening meal might include cold meats, scrambled eggs, bacon, salad, cakes, and fruit, served alongside the all important cuppa.

One must dress for the occasion of afternoon tea in the palm court at the Ritz Hotel in London. The carefully trained staff pours Earl Grey or Darjeeling tea from an elegant silver service and offers finger sandwiches of smoked salmon on dark bread, watercress and cheddar cheese, and egg salad. Scones, cakes, and petits fours with whipped and clotted cream complete the sumptuous, time-honored repast.

English Tea-Time Sandwiches

INVENTED BY THE EARL OF SANDWICH IN THE EIGHTEENTH CENTURY, THE ENGLISH TEA-TIME SANDWICH HAS BECOME A WELL-ESTABLISHED TRADITION.

IT IS FAR BETTER TO USE BREAD THAT IS A DAY OLD, FOR TO OBTAIN THE REALLY ELEGANT ENGLISH TEA-TIME SANDWICH IT IS NECESSARY TO USE VERY THINLY SLICED BREAD — EITHER WHITE OR BROWN, AND REMOVE CRUSTS ONCE THE SANDWICHES HAVE BEEN FILLED.

TEA MENUS HAVE INCLUDED SANDWICHES WITH SPREADS OF: CUCUMBER, WATERCRESS AND CREAM CHEESE, CHICKEN OR EGG SALAD, LOBSTER, SHRIMP, SMOKED SALMON, SARDINES, ANCHOVIES, VARIOUS HARD OR SEMI-SOFT CHEESES, CREAM CHEESE WITH CHIVES OR CANDIED GINGER. THE FILLINGS AND SPREADS ARE ENDLESS AND YOU CAN HAVE FUN USING EVERY KIND OF BREAD — BLACK, BROWN, WHITE, RYE, WHOLE WHEAT, PUMPERNICKEL AND BREADS MADE WITH FRUIT AND CHEESE.

THE TEA SANDWICH IS USUALLY BITE SIZE AND CRUSTLESS, BUT EVEN HERE YOU CAN BE FREEWHEELING AND INNOVATE. WE HAPPEN TO LIKE CRUST AND ABHOR THE WASTE OF IT.

THE MORE ATTRACTIVE AND UNUSUAL TEA SANDWICHES ARE, THE MORE APPEALING WILL BE THE WHOLE TEA EXPERIENCE. MY PERSONAL PASSION IS CAVIAR ON TOAST POINTS!

Rose Petal Honey

1 CUP UNSPRAYED ROSE PETALS, PREFERABLY THE FRAGRANT OLD-FASHIONED TYPES

1 CUP HONEY

RINSE THE ROSE PETALS BRIEFLY IN COLD WATER; DRY IN A SALAD SPINNER. IN A NONALUMINUM PAN, SLOWLY HEAT THE HONEY UNTIL RUNNY. STIR IN THE ROSE PETALS WITH A WOODEN SPOON, COVER, AND STEEP OVER LOWEST HEAT FOR 45 MINUTES, STIRRING OCCASIONALLY. TURN OFF THE HEAT AND LET COOL 15 MINUTES. POUR THE HONEY THROUGH A FINE SIEVE INTO A STERILIZED JAR. RESERVE THE "HONEY" ROSE PETALS TO FLAVOR ICE CREAM, MUSTARDS, BAKED GOODS, AND CHUTNEYS.

Lemon Butter

ONE OF THE MOST DELECTABLE SPREADS FOR TOAST IS LEMON CURD OR LEMON BUTTER. EXCELLENT COMMERCIAL BRANDS ARE AVAILABLE, BUT NOTHING WILL COMPARE WITH FRESH LEMON BUTTER YOU MAKE YOURSELF. IT KEEPS WELL AND GOES HAPPILY ON EVERYTHING FROM TOAST TO WAFFLES AS WELL AS ON TARTS AND AS FILLING FOR LAYER CAKES. IT'S AS GOOD AS HAVING LEMON MERINGUE PIE WITHOUT THE MERINGUE AND CRUST!

3 EGGS, 1 CUP SUGAR, 5 TABLESPOONS MELTED BUTTER, JUICE AND GRATED RIND OF 2 LEMONS. BEAT THE EGGS AND ADD THE SUGAR GRADUALLY, CONTINUING TO BEAT. ADD THE BUTTER, LEMON JUICE AND RIND. COOK IN DOUBLE BOILER UNTIL THICKENED, STIRRING CONSTANTLY. LET COOL AND STORE IN REFRIGERATOR.

Devonshire Splits

TRADITIONALLY THESE LITTLE BUNS ARE SERVED WITH CLOTTED CREAM AND HOME-MADE STRAWBERRY JAM. SERVED WITH A POT OF TEA THIS WOULD BE CALLED A CREAM TEA IN ENGLAND'S WEST COUNTRY.

4½ CUPS BREAD FLOUR
½ TSP SALT
2 TSP ACTIVE DRY YEAST
1 TSP SUGAR
2 TBSP MELTED BUTTER
1¼ CUPS WARM MILK

SIEVE THE FLOUR AND SALT INTO A MIXING BOWL. HEAT THE MILK UNTIL TEPID, STIR IN THE SUGAR AND SPRINKLE THE YEAST ON TOP. LEAVE IN A WARM PLACE FOR 15 MINUTES, WHEN IT SHOULD BE FROTHY. MAKE A WELL IN THE CENTER OF THE FLOUR, POUR IN THE YEAST LIQUID AND MELTED BUTTER AND USING A WOODEN SPOON MIX TO A SOFT DOUGH. TURN ONTO A FLOURED BOARD AND KNEAD FOR 8-10 MINUTES. PUT IN A CLEAN BOWL, COVER WITH PLASTIC WRAP AND LEAVE TO STAND UNTIL DOUBLED IN SIZE.

CUT THE DOUGH INTO 12 EVEN-SIZED PIECES, KNEAD EACH PIECE INTO A BALL, FLATTEN INTO A ROUND ABOUT ½ INCH THICK AND PLACE ON A LIGHTLY GREASED AND WARMED BAKING SHEET. COVER WITH A CLOTH AND LET STAND IN A WARM PLACE FOR 20 MINUTES.

BAKE AT 425°F FOR 15-20 MINUTES. REMOVE FROM THE OVEN AND COOL ON A WIRE RACK, BEFORE SPLITTING AND SPREADING WITH CLOTTED CREAM AND STRAWBERRY JAM.

Northumberland 'Singin' Hinny'

THESE LITTLE FLAT CAKES MAKE A 'SINGING' NOISE AS THEY COOK ON THE GRIDDLE, AND THE WORD 'HINNY' IS A TERM OF ENDEARMENT USUALLY USED BY MOTHERS IN THE NORTH OF ENGLAND WHEN SPEAKING TO YOUNG CHILDREN WHO, WHEN WAITING FOR THEIR TEAS, WOULD PESTER THEIR MOTHERS AS TO WHETHER IT WAS READY OR NOT, AND AS THE LITTLE CAKES WOULD BE COOKING AWAY SHE WOULD ANSWER THEM BY SAYING, 'NO, NO, THEY'RE NOT READY YET, JUST SINGIN', HINNY.'

4 TBSP BUTTER

2½ CUPS SELF-RISING FLOUR

1 TSP SALT

4 TBSP. SUPERFINE SUGAR

6 TBSP CURRANTS

3/4 CUP HALF-AND-HALF

SIEVE THE FLOUR AND SALT INTO A LARGE MIXING BOWL, CUT THE BUTTER INTO THE FLOUR USING YOUR FINGERTIPS, AND STIR IN THE SUGAR AND CURRANTS. MAKE A WELL IN THE CENTER, AND POUR IN THE HALF-AND-HALF. WITH A WOODEN SPOON SLOWLY DRAW THE DRY INGREDIENTS INTO THE LIQUID TO FORM A SOFT DOUGH. ROLL THE DOUGH OUT ON A LIGHTLY FLOURED BOARD TO ABOUT ¼ INCH THICK AND PRICK ALL OVER WITH A FORK. CUT INTO QUARTERS AND PLACE ON A MODERATELY HOT GRIDDLE AND COOK FOR ABOUT 4 MINUTES EACH SIDE, UNTIL NICELY BROWNED. SERVE HOT, CUT IN TWO AND BUTTERED.

$\mathcal{T}$EA TIME LINE

CIRCA 2700 B.C.   CHINESE EMPEROR SHEN NUNG DISCOVERS TEA.

CIRCA 725 B.C.   T'ANG DYNASTY: CH'A, THE DISTINCTIVE CHINESE IDEOGRAPH FOR TEA, FIRST APPEARS. THE EVOLUTION OF THE CHARACTER DEMONSTRATES THE SIGNIFICANCE OF TEA IN DAILY LIFE.

805 A.D.   DENGO DAISHI, BUDDHIST PATRON SAINT OF JAPANESE TEA, INTRODUCES TEA-GROWING IN JAPAN.

1191   AFTER CENTURIES OF NEGLECT, THE CULTIVATION OF TEA IN JAPAN IS REVIVED BY THE BUDDHIST ABBOT YESAI, WHO SUBSEQUENTLY PUBLISHES THE FIRST JAPANESE TEA BOOK. HIS FRIEND AND BROTHER, ABBOT MYO-E, PIONEERS THE FAMOUS UJI TEA-GROWING DISTRICT IN 1200.

1500   MING DYNASTY: IN IMITATION OF SPOUTED EARTHENWARE WINE EWERS, THE FIRST TEAPOTS WERE MADE AT YI-XANG, A SPOT NEAR SHANGHAI FAMOUS FOR ITS CLAYS. BLACK, GREEN, AND OOLONG, THE THREE FORMS OF CONTEMPORARY TEA, BECOME PREVALENT.

1610   TEA REACHES EUROPE FOR THE FIRST TIME, CARRIED BY THE DUTCH FROM A TRADING STATION IN BANTAM, JAVA. THEY BUY TEA FROM CHINESE MERCHANTS, WHO SPEAK THE AMOY DIALECT AND THEREFORE REFER TO THE PRODUCT AS "TEA."

1623   THE FIRST ANNUAL PUBLIC JAPANESE TEA RITUAL, KNOWN AS THE "TEA JOURNEY," IS HELD.

1657   GARWAY'S COFFEE HOUSE IN LONDON HOLDS ITS FIRST PUBLIC SALE OF TEA. GARWAY'S STARTS TO ADVERTISE THE "VERTUES OF THE LEAF THEA."

1680

MADAME DE LA SABLIERE, WIFE OF THE FRENCH POET, INTRODUCES FRANCE TO THE CUSTOM OF DRINKING TEA WITH MILK. POURING THE MILK INTO THE CUP OF HOT TEA COOLED THE TEA SLIGHTLY, MAKING IT LESS APT TO BREAK HER CHERISHED EGGSHELL PORCELAIN TEA CUPS.

1773

ON DECEMBER 16 AT THE BOSTON TEA PARTY, AMERICAN COLONISTS DUMP THE ENTIRE BOSTON CONSIGNMENT OF THE JOHN COMPANY'S TEA INTO THE HARBOR IN PROTEST OF THE EXORBITANT TEA TAX.

1856

THE FIRST TEA IS PLANTED IN THE DARJEELING DISTRICT OF NORTHERN INDIA.

1900

THE LAST CAMEL CARAVAN CARRYING TEA DEPARTS PEKING FOR RUSSIA. DURING THE SAME YEAR, THE LAST LINK OF THE TRANS-SIBERIAN RAILROAD IS COMPLETED.

1904

DUE TO THE UNBEARABLE HEAT, ICED TEA IS INVENTED AT THE ST. LOUIS WORLD'S FAIR. DR. SHEPARD'S SOUTH CAROLINA GROWN TEA WINS "BEST IN SHOW" MEDAL.

1908

MR. WILLIAM SULLIVAN, TEA MERCHANT IN NEW YORK, INADVERTENTLY INVENTS THE TEA BAG.

1925

AFRICA PASSES THE MILLION-POUND MARK IN TEA SHIPMENTS. BROOKE BOND BEGINS BUYING LAND AND PLANTING TEA IN KENYA.

1958

THREE HUNDRED YEARS AFTER CHINA TEA WAS FIRST INTRODUCED TO ENGLAND, IT IS SOLD THERE FOR THE FIRST TIME BY ITS CHINESE PRODUCERS.

Lazing in a shady hammock, many grown-ups have reported observing that children know that fairies enjoy their own tea parties. Snapdragons stand guard and bees hum a cappella as the fairies feast on birchbark toast slathered with honeysuckle jelly. Dewdrop tea is served in acorn tea cups.

Fairy tea party: moss tablecloth, dainty leaf napkins, twig furniture, and "flower fairy doll" with flower wardrobe, etc.

Summer

*I*SOTONIC TEAS HAVE ADDED NATURAL SALTS AND VITAMINS WHICH NEED TO BE REPLACED FREQUENTLY ON THOSE ACTIVE, HOT SUMMER DAYS.

*S*ECRET FAIRY MESSAGES ARE PAINTED ON PAPER WITH LEMON JUICE. TO DECODE THE MAGICAL MISSIVES, ADULTS QUICKLY PASS A HOT IRON OVER THE PAPER WHILE ASTONISHED CHILDREN WIGGLE WITH CURIOSITY!

Recipe For Fuzzy Fairy Iced Tea:

SPARKLING WATER, TEA, AND FRUIT JUICE SPLASHED TOGETHER OVER ICE JEWELS. MAKE THESE GEMS GLITTER BY PLACING LEMON SLICES, BERRIES, OR FRESH MINT LEAVES IN ICE CUBE TRAYS AND FILLING THEM WITH FAIRY TEA.

Hamburg-Amerika Linie

WHY, THERE'S PLENTY OF ROOM!

CHILDREN CAN FORM WHEAT BREAD INTO SHAPES WITH LARGE COOKIE CUTTERS. STARS, ANIMALS, HEARTS, AND SO ON. FILL OR STACK THE SHAPED SLICES WITH WHATEVER SEASONAL BOUNTY IS AT HAND: CUCUMBERS, AVOCADOS, TOMATOES, CREAM CHEESE, TEA JELLY, FRUIT JAM, BUTTER BEATEN WITH CINNAMON AND A DROP OF VANILLA...

AND DON'T FORGET FLOWERS FOR THE TABLE.

COME FOR TEA

"DO YOU WANT YOUR ADVENTURE NOW", PETER SAID CASUALLY TO JOHN, "OR WOULD YOU LIKE TO HAVE YOUR TEA FIRST?" WENDY SAID, "TEA FIRST, QUICKLY."

PETER PAN   J.M. BARRIE, 1904

NEVER-NEVER LAND COULD WAIT, BUT REAL CHILDREN CAN NEVER WAIT FOR THEIR OWN HIGH TEA. THE MORE POURING, SLOSHING, AND GIGGLING THE BETTER. SCALED DOWN FURNITURE AND TOT-SIZED TEA SETS MEAN BIG TIME FUN.

TRY TEPID MINT, CHAMOMILE, FENNEL, OR LICORICE TEA. IN THE SUMMER OFFER TEA ICED OR SPICED WITH HERBS OR SLICES OF FRUIT, SUCH AS ORANGES AND APPLES. (GREAT FOR MUNCHING ON AFTER ALL THE TEA IS GONE.)

SERVE WITH "WE MADE 'EM OURSELVES" TEA SANDWICHES.

A TEMPEST IN A TEAPOT, TWO ICE CUBES IN A GLASS.

In the early eighteenth century, American colonists were avid tea drinkers. The Puritans drank theirs bitter, black, and salted, while other New Englanders preferred green China tea tinted with saffron and scented with iris root or gardenia petals.

1973 Series
COMMEMORATING The
BOSTON TEA PARTY
AMERICAN REVOLUTION BICENTENNIAL

Spirit of '76

THOMAS HUTCHINSON - ROYAL GOVERNOR OF BOSTON (1771-1774) - REFUSED TEA SHIPS TO CLEAR BOSTON HARBOR RESULTING IN BOSTON TEA PARTY

Sherwood

OFFICIAL First Day Cover

BOSTON, MA JUL 4 1973

FIRST DAY OF ISSUE

Tea was the third most imported product in the colonies after textiles and manufactured goods. When England found itself financially drained from the French and Indian wars, Parliament levied a heavy tax on tea. The colonists' ensuing boycott of tea culminated in the Boston Tea Party, at which protestors threw the entire contents of a British tea shipment into the harbor. It and many other similar tea parties fanned the flames of revolution and made coffee drinkers of Americans.

On April 18, 1775, two years after the infamous party, a silversmith named Paul Revere, who specialized in making silver teapots, climbed to the top of the highest steeple in Lexington, Massachusetts, to hang warning lanterns that alerted rebel colonists to the advance of British troops: "ONE IF BY LAND AND TWO IF BY SEA." Tea had helped to start a revolution.

REVERE'S DEMOCRATIC FERVOR INSPIRED HIM TO CREATE "THE PATRIOTIC TEAPOT," WHICH ABANDONED THE ROCOCO EXCESSES OF THE BRITISH IN FAVOR OF CLEAN, SOBER LINES.

ONE SWELTERING DAY AT THE 1904 ST. LOUIS WORLD'S FAIR, A TEA DEALER NAMED MR. RICHARD BLECHYNDEN WAS ATTEMPTING TO INTRODUCE THE AMERICAN PUBLIC TO THEN LITTLE-KNOWN INDIAN TEAS. BLECHYNDEN HIMSELF SHRANK FROM THE IDEA OF HOT TEA AND WAS NOT HAVING MUCH SUCCESS ATTRACTING CUSTOMERS. TO REFRESH HIMSELF, HE SLIPPED TWO ICE CUBES INTO HIS GLASS; ICED TEA WAS AN INSTANT HIT. TODAY, MORE AMERICANS PROBABLY DRINK THEIR TEA ICED RATHER THAN HOT.

TEA BAGS, ANOTHER AMERICAN INNOVATION, WERE THE BRIGHT IDEA OF NEW YORK TEA MERCHANT THOMAS SULLIVAN, WHO STITCHED UP TINY SILK SACHETS OF TEA TO SERVE AS SAMPLES FOR THE CONVENIENCE OF HIS CLIENTS.

HIGH-TECH TEAS NOW INCLUDE INSTANT VERSIONS MADE FROM FREEZE-DRIED CRYSTALS. FOR THOSE DESPERATE FOR A NIP ON THE RUN, THERE IS CANNED AND BOTTLED ICED TEA.

TAY AMOY DIALECT TSA ANNAMESE SHAI ARABIAN CH'A CANTONESE TE CZECHOSLOVAK

Tasters' Glossary

"Its taste is perhaps the subtlest the tongue can experience, so unassertive it can be almost subliminal. Tea both calms and stimulates, but its secret teaching is conscious enjoyment."

NORWOOD PRATT, TEA EMPORIUM

Bakey
HAVING AN UNPLEASANT TASTE DUE TO FIRING THE LEAF AT AN ELEVATED TEMPERATURE. "BAKEY" IS NOT AS STRONG AS "BURNT."

Body
THE VISCOSITY OF A TEA WITH "BODY" MAY BE CONSIDERED "FULL" OR "LIGHT."

Burnt
DESCRIBES EXTREMELY OVER-FIRED TEA.

Character
AROMA AND FLAVOR ASSOCIATED WITH A CERTAIN REGION, DISTRICT, OR GARDEN OF ORIGIN.

Chesty
MAINTAINING A RESINOUS ODOR IMPARTED BY INFERIOR OR UNSEASONED PACKING MATERIALS.

Common
VERY LIGHT, THIN, AND PLAIN, WITH NO DISTINCT FLAVOR.

Complex
CONTAINING A HARMONIOUS MIX OF VARIOUS FLAVORS CHARACTERISTIC OF ONLY THE VERY FINEST TEAS.

TE HUNGARIAN TE ITALIAN AND SPANISH CHA JAPANESE TA KOREAN TEJA LATVIAN TE MALAYAN

E DANISH **THEE** DUTCH AND GERMAN **TEA** ENGLISH **TEE** FINNISH **THE** FRENCH **CHA** HINDU

Fresh — RECENTLY MANUFACTURED, TEA THAT HAS BEEN STORED ON THE SHELF TOO RECENTLY TO BECOME STALE.

Gone off — SPOILED BY IMPROPER STORAGE OR PACKING, OR SIMPLY PAST ITS PRIME AND THUS STALE.

Mature — DESCRIBES FULLY FERMENTED BLACK TEAS.

Peak — THE HIGH POINT OF THE TASTING EXPERIENCE WHEN, MOMENTS AFTER THE BREW, OR LIQUOR, ENTERS THE MOUTH, ITS BODY, FLAVOR, AND PUNGENCY ARE FULLY APPRECIATED.

Pointy — SHOWING A DESIRABLE PROPERTY, SUCH AS BRISKNESS OR FINE FRAGRANCE.

Pungent — ASTRINGENT, WITH A GOOD COMBINATION OF BRIGHTNESS AND STRENGTH.

Self-drinking — HAVING SUFFICIENT AROMA, FLAVOR, BODY, AND COLOR TO STAND ALONE.

Strength — DESCRIBES A TEA WITH SUBSTANCE.

E NORWEGIAN **CHA** PERSIAN **CHA** PORTUGUESE **CHAI** RUSSIAN **TE** SWEDISH **TEY** TAMILIAN **CHAY** TURKISH

I HAVE FAVORITE TEA EMPORIUMS FROM THIS COAST TO THAT AND
WELL BEYOND. BUT I DO WONDER WHETHER THE MOST EXOTIC TEA WOULD
NOT BE AT A PICNIC ATOP THE GREAT WALL OF CHINA? SOMEDAY?

*Y*OUR FAVORITE PLACES

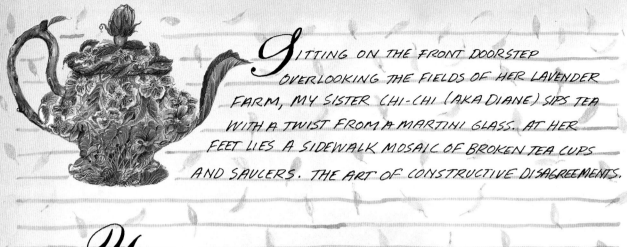

Sitting on the front doorstep overlooking the fields of her lavender farm, my sister Chi-Chi (aka Diane) sips tea with a twist from a martini glass. At her feet lies a sidewalk mosaic of broken tea cups and saucers. The art of constructive disagreements.

Your favorite places

In my family, the first bite of any seasonal fruit entitles you to make a wish. I look forward to the season's first strawberries, dipped in crème fraiche. Last year, my strawberry wish was for a brunch of Russian Caravan Tea, blinis with caviar and smoked salmon to celebrate the first strawberries of the next season.

Your favorite recipes for spring

In Atlanta, a glass half-full of ice tea is really half empty. The denizens of "Hotlanta" know how to top it off with a half glass of lemonade to make the most refreshing combo in the South.

Your favorite recipes for summer

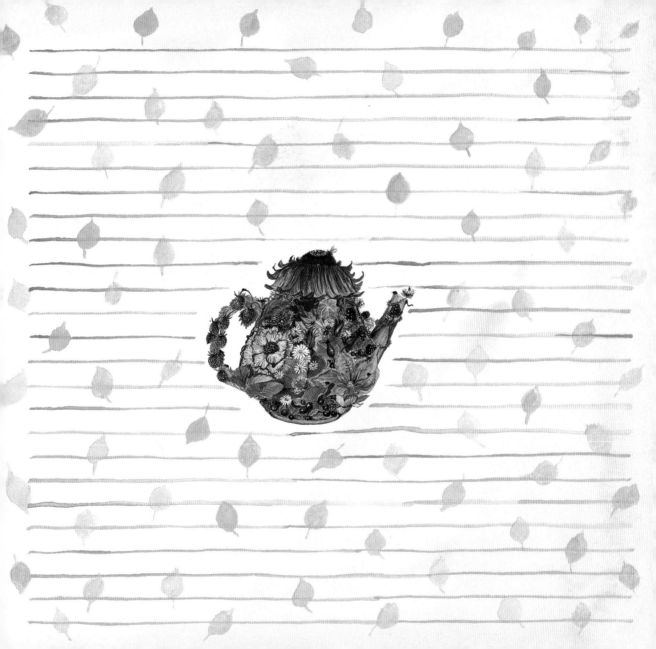

*O*NE ASPECT OF NESTS, EGGS, AND SEASHELLS THAT FASCINATES ME IS THAT THEY ARE ALL CONTAINERS OF SORTS, DESIGNED TO HOLD GREAT TREASURES. THE AUTUMN HARVEST YIELDS MINIATURE PUMPKINS IN WHICH TO SERVE EDIBLE TREASURES. SCOOP OUT THE PULP AND FILL WITH CURRY PUMPKIN SOUP, SUCCOTASH, OR GINGER ICE CREAM. THESE DELIGHTS ARE HOT, HOT WITH CHANDERNAGOR TEA, A FRENCH TEA IN THE COLONIAL INDIAN STYLE, PREPARED WITH PEPPER, CARDAMOM, CLOVES, AND MORE!

*Y*OUR FAVORITE RECIPES FOR AUTUMN

'*T*IS THE SEASON FOR SPICED, AND SOMETIMES SPIKED, TEA CIDER (HOT APPLE CIDER, ORANGE PEKOE TEA, CINNAMON, CLOVES, AND BRANDY,) TO ENJOY WHILE BAKING A FLOCK OF GINGERBREAD BIRDS FOR DECORATING THE CHRISTMAS TREE.

*Y*OUR FAVORITE RECIPES FOR WINTER

*M*Y HUMBLE THANKS FOR ALL THE GREAT HELP AND ENCOURAGEMENT I RECEIVE ON THESE BOOKS FROM FAMILY AND FRIENDS AND IN PARTICULAR...

...THE LOVELY AND TALENTED LADIES OF COLLINS PUBLISHERS SAN FRANCISCO WHO WORKED ESPECIALLY HARD ON THIS BOOK: JENNIFER BARRY, MAURA CAREY DAMACION, JULIE BERNATZ, DAYNA MACY, KARI PERIN, AND MORE "JENNIFERS" THAN ONE CAN SHAKE A TEASPOON AT INCLUDING JENNIFER WARD, JENNIFER COLLINS, AND JENNIFER GRACE!

...TO JONATHAN MILLS OF COLLINS PUBLISHERS ALSO FOR HIS BRILLIANT ATTENTION TO VERY TRICKY PRODUCTION DETAILS--ESPECIALLY ON THESE BOOKS.

...TO SHELLEI ADDISON FOR HER WONDERFUL TEXT CONTRIBUTIONS AND TO ALL OF HER EDITORIAL ARTS CREW AT FLYING FISH BOOKS.

...TO MY DAUGHTERS SUNNY AND WENDY KOCH FOR THEIR INCREDIBLE ASSISTANCE ON DESIGN AND LAYOUT AND MK GRAPHICS BUSINESS.

...TO OUR MANY FRIENDS WHO SUPPLIED BEAUTIFUL TEA ACCESSORIES, BOOKS AND INFORMATION INCLUDING STEVE FLETCHER AND CARL CROFT OF TAMPOPO INC., MY SISTER DIANE AND HER HUSBAND GARY MEEHAN OF BONNY DOON FARM, DAPHNE DERVEN, JILL HAMILTON, ANNETTE MOELLER, ELIZABETH FADER AND DON GUY.

...AND ONCE AGAIN, TO MY RELENTLESS PARTNER AND DEAR FRIEND, KRISTIN JOYCE, WHO HAS STARED INTO MANY CUPS OF MARCO POLO TEA AND SEEN BOOK AFTER BOOK APPEAR BEFORE HER EYES! WE AWAIT THE DAY WHEN WE CAN ACTUALLY SIT A SPELL, SUP A CUP, AND RELISH THESE DELECTABLE BOOKS!